THE FIRST NOEL

PICTURES BY **JANINA DOMANSKA**

GREENWILLOW BOOKS, NEW YORK

Watercolor paints, colored dyes,
and black ink were used in
the full-color paintings.
The text type is ITC Galliard and
the display type is Caslon Openface.

Printed in Hong Kong
by South China Printing Co.
Printed in the United States of America
First Edition 1 2 3 4 5 6 7 8 9 10

Library of Congress Cataloging-in-Publication Data
Domanska, Janina.
The first Noel.
Summary: Full page illustrations with the
text of the well-known Christmas carol
present the story of the night Jesus was born.
1. Carols—Texts. 2. Jesus Christ—Nativity—
Songs and music—Texts. 3. Christmas music.
[1. Carols. 2. Christmas music.
3. Jesus Christ—Nativity] I. Title.
PZ8.3.D698Fi 1986 763.6'5 85-27084
ISBN 0-688-04324-0
ISBN 0-688-04325-9 (lib. bdg.)

FOR SUSAN HIRSCHMAN, WITH LOVE

The first Noel the Angel did say
Was to certain poor shepherds in fields as they lay.

In fields where they lay keeping their sheep,
On a cold winter's night that was so deep:

Noel, Noel, Noel, Noel,

Born is the King of Israel.

They looked up and saw a star,
Shining in the east, beyond them far.

And to the earth it gave great light,
And so it continued both day and night:

Noel, Noel, Noel, Noel,

Born is the King of Israel.

And by the light of that same star,
Three Wise Men came from country far.

To seek for a king was their intent,
And to follow the star wherever it went:

Noel, Noel, Noel, Noel,

Born is the King of Israel.

This star drew nigh to the northwest,
O'er Bethlehem it took its rest.

And there it did both stop and stay,
Right over the place where Jesus lay:

Noel, Noel, Noel, Noel,

Born is the King of Israel.

Then entered in those Wise Men three,
Full reverently upon their knee.

And offered there, in his presence,
Their gold and myrrh and frankincense:

Noel, Noel, Noel, Noel,

Born is the King of Israel.

THE FIRST NOEL

English Traditional Song

Arranged by John Krumich